VINCENT VAN GOGH

Chronicle Books · San Francisco

Asnières, la Grande Jatte! 1886 was the heyday of boating, and Vincent, like Seurat and the other painters, was drawn to the great island, where he painted the popular weekend restaurants, the boats and the open-air cafés decked with flags.

Above all, of course, it was the merry and fashionable boating throng who made Asnières resound with their shouts and laughter. Here they disembarked with fanfares, accompanied by their girls wearing the sailor suits, English berets and billowing skirts and bustles of the period; and all day long this flotilla would yell in anticipation of cavorting at the Sirène dance-hall. Throughout the evening the cafés swarmed with these revellers. Vincent, meanwhile, had to make do with painting or sketching the exteriors of these temples of revelry, which reached its highest pitch under Gratiot's arbours. He hardly ever went in, except to Père Perruchot's modest restaurant, where you could enjoy a bottle of cheap wine from the slopes of Suresnes.

Gustave Coquiot, *Vincent van Gogh*, 1923

THE RESTAURANT DE LA SIRÈNE AT ASNIÈRES, 1887

I think I shall end by not feeling lonely in the house, and that during the bad days in the winter for instance, and the long evenings, I shall find some occupation that will take all my attention. Weavers and basket makers often spend whole seasons alone or almost alone, with their occupation for their only distraction.

But what makes these people stay in one place is precisely the feeling of domesticity, the *reassuring familiar look of things*. I should certainly like company, but if I have not got it, I shall not be unhappy because of that, and then too the time will come when I shall have someone. I have little doubt of it.

Letter to his brother Theo, September 1888

ROMANS PARISIENS (THE YELLOW BOOKS), 1887

His was a restless, tormented mind, full of inspired ideas, vague and ardent, drawn perpetually towards the summits where the mysteries of human life reveal themselves. One never knew what force was active inside him – whether it was the apostle or the artist; he did not even know himself . . .

He was not absorbed by nature either. He had absorbed nature into himself; he had forced it to unbend, to mould itself into the shapes of his thoughts, to follow him in his flights, even to submit to his highly characteristic deformations . . .

He spares himself no effort, to the benefit of the trees, skies, flowers, fields, which he inflates with the astonishing dream of his being. And how he has understood too how much sadness, how much that lies unrevealed, how much divinity there is in the eyes of the poor and his brother invalids.

Octave Mirbeau, *L'Echo de Paris*, 31 March 1891

THE BUSHES, 1888

I must warn you that everyone will think that I work too fast. Don't believe a word of it. Is it not emotion, the sincerity of one's feeling for nature, that draws us? And if these emotions are sometimes so strong that one works without knowing one does so, when sometimes the brush strokes come with a sequence and a coherence like words in a speech or in a letter, then one must remember that it has not always been so, and that in time to come there will again be dreary days, devoid of inspiration. So one must strike while the iron is hot . . .

Letter to Theo, July 1888

CARAVANS, 1888

Here is a sketch of a sower: large ploughed field with clods of earth, for the most part frankly violet. A field of ripe wheat, yellow ochre in tone with a little carmine. The sky, chrome yellow, almost as bright as the sun itself, which is chrome yellow No. 1 with a little white, whereas the rest of the sky is chrome yellow Nos. 1 and 2 mixed. So very yellow. The sower's shirt is blue and his trousers white. Size 25 canvas, square.

Letter to Theo, June 1888

To begin with, I found everywhere a disorder that shocked me. His box of colours was scarcely large enough to contain all the squeezed tubes which were never closed, yet in spite of all this disorder, this mess, there was something brilliant in his canvases; in his words too. His Dutch brain was afire with the Bible. In Arles, the quays, the bridges, and the boats, in fact all of the *Midi* became Holland to him. He even forgot how to write Dutch . . . From the first month I saw our joint finances take on the same aspects of disorder. What was to be done? The situation was delicate, the cash-box being modestly filled by his brother . . . Only with great precaution and much coaxing, little in keeping with my character, did I refer to the matter. I must admit that I succeeded much more easily than I had expected.

Paul Gauguin, *Avant et Après*, 1923

LE PONT DE L'ANGLOIS, 1888

Vincent, at the time of my arrival at Arles, was up to his ears in the neo-impressionist school, and he was floundering considerably, which made him unhappy. Not that this school, like all schools, was bad, but because it was not in harmony with his impatient and independent nature. With all his yellows and violets, all this work with complementaries – a disorderly work on his part – he only achieved soft, incomplete, and monotonous harmonies; the sound of the bugle was lacking. I undertook the task of explaining things to him, which was easy for me, for I found a rich and fruitful ground. Like all original natures marked with the stamp of personality, Vincent was without distrust or obstinacy. From that day Van Gogh made astonishing progress; he seemed to become aware of everything that was in him, and thence came all the series of sunflowers after sunflowers in brilliant sunshine.

Paul Gauguin, *Avant et Après*, 1923

THE DANCE HALL AT ARLES, 1888

My dear Theo,

I wrote to you already, early this morning, then I went away to go on with a picture of a garden in sunshine. Then I brought it back and went out again with a blank canvas, and that also is finished. And now I want to write to you again.

Nature here is so extraordinarily beautiful! Everywhere and over all the vault of the sky is a marvellous blue, and the sun sheds a radiance of pale sulphur; it is as soft and lovely as the combination of celestial blues and yellows in Vermeer's paintings. I cannot paint it as beautifully as that, but it absorbs me so much that I let myself go without thinking of any rules.

Letter to Theo, September 1888

My dear Theo,

I am writing to you from Saintes-Maries on the shore of the Mediterranean at last. The Mediterranean has the colouring of mackerel, changeable I mean. You don't always know if it is green or violet, you can't even say it's blue, because the next moment the changing reflection has taken on a tinge of rose or grey . . .

One night I went for a walk by the sea along the empty shore. It was not gay, but neither was it sad – it was – beautiful. The deep blue sky was flecked with clouds of a blue deeper than the fundamental blue of intense cobalt, and others of a clearer blue, like the blue whiteness of the Milky Way. In the blue depth the stars were sparkling, greenish, yellow, white, rose, brighter, flashing more like jewels, than they do at home – even in Paris: opals you might call them, emeralds, lapis, rubies, sapphires.

The sea was a very deep ultramarine – the shore a sort of violet and faint russet as I saw it, and on the dunes (about seventeen feet high they are) some bushes of Prussian blue . . .

Letter to Theo, June 1888

SAILING BOATS AT SAINTES-MARIES, 1888

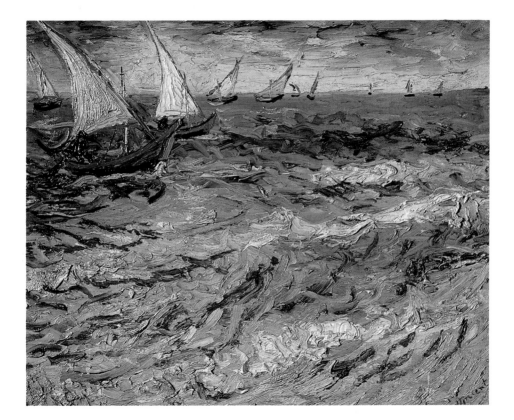

All his work is characterized by its excess, an excessive force, an excessive nervous tension, a violence in expression. In his categorical affirmation of the nature of things, in the boldness with which his forms are often simplified, in the insolence with which he stares into the face of the sun, in the fiery vehemence of his drawing and colour, even in the smallest details of his technique, he reveals himself as powerful, masculine, daring, very often brutal and sometimes ingenuously delicate . . .

Lastly, and above all, he is a hyper-aesthete, perceiving with abnormal, perhaps even painful intensity the scarcely perceptible, secret characteristics of line and form, and still more of colour . . . That is why his realism, the realism of this neurotic, and his sincerity and his truth are different from the realism, the sincerity and truth of those great *petits bourgeois* of Holland, so sound of body and well-balanced in mind, who were his fathers and his masters.

Albert Aurier, 'Les Isoles. Vincent Van Gogh', in *Mercure de France*, January 1890

WHEATFIELD WITH SETTING SUN, 1888

For today I am all right again. My eyes are still tired, but then I had a new idea in my head and here is the sketch of it. Another canvas of size 30. This time it's just simply my bedroom, only here colour is to do everything, and giving by its simplification a grander style to things, is to be suggestive here of *rest* or of sleep in general. In a word, looking at the picture ought to rest the brain, or rather the imagination. The walls are pale violet. The floor is red tiles. The wood of the bed and chairs is the yellow of fresh butter, the sheets and pillows very light greenish-citron. The coverlet scarlet. The window green. The toilet table orange, the basin blue. The doors lilac. And that is all – there is nothing in this room with its closed shutters. The broad lines of the furniture again must express inviolable rest. Portraits on the walls, and a mirror and a towel and some clothes. The frame – as there is no white in the picture – will be white.

This by way of revenge for the enforced rest I have been obliged to take.

Letter to Theo, October 1888

VINCENT'S BEDROOM, ARLES, 1889

But for the rest, painting and, in my opinion, especially the painting of rural life, gives serenity, though one may have all kinds of worries and miseries on the surface of life. I mean painting is a *home* and one does not experience that homesickness, that peculiar feeling Hennebeau had . . .

And I was sick of the *boredom* of civilization. It *is* better, one *is* happier if one carries it out – literally though – one feels at least that one is really alive. And it is a good thing in winter to be deep in the snow, in the autumn deep in the yellow leaves, in summer among the ripe corn, in spring amid the grass; it is a good thing to be always with the mowers and the peasant girls, in summer with a big sky overhead, in winter by the fireside, and to feel that it always has been and always will be so.

Letter to Theo, June 1885

THE SIESTA, 1890

Vincent arrived at Auvers on 21 May and went straight to visit Dr Gachet. The doctor had a practice in Paris for a few days each week, and spent the rest of the time engraving and painting in the Oise. He owned paintings by Cézanne, Pissarro and Monet, and took a passionate interest in the experiments and triumphs of post-impressionism . . .

Vincent quickly settled in and, pleased with the softer light and the greenness of the landscape, got down to work. The little valleys and gardens of the Ile de France, with their gentle and soft lines, the light, rustling trees, the tranquil charm of its tumbledown cottages and clusters of villages. The calming phase begun at Saint-Rémy is now brought to fulfilment, and the respect shown in his use of colour matches that of Daubigny, whose paintings had made the name of Auvers-sur-Oise some thirty years earlier. The harsh depiction of objects, people and landscapes in the south, executed with bold strokes against metallic backgrounds, is succeeded here by the painting of atmosphere.

Paul Colin, *Van Gogh*, 1925

THE COTTAGES, 1890

I hope to send you a portrait of him [Dr Gachet] soon. Then I have painted two studies at his house, which I gave him last week, an aloe with marigolds and cypresses, then last Sunday some white roses, vines and a white figure in it.

I shall most probably also do the portrait of his daughter, who is nineteen years old, and with whom I imagine Jo would soon be friends.

. . . Now nothing, absolutely nothing, is keeping us here but Gachet – but he will remain a friend, I should think. I feel that I can do not too bad a picture every time I go to his house, and he will continue to ask me to dinner every Sunday or Monday.

Letter to Theo, June 1890

MLLE GACHET IN THE GARDEN, 1890

Auvers is quite beautiful – many thatched roofs, among others, something that is becoming rather scarce . . . It is of a grave beauty, the real countryside, characteristic and picturesque.

I am totally absorbed by that immense plain covered with fields of wheat which extends beyond the hillside; it is wide as the sea, of a subtle yellow, a subtle tender green, with the subtle violet of a ploughed and weeded patch and with neatly delineated green spots of potato fields in bloom. All this under a sky of delicate colours, blue and white and pink and purple. For the time being I am calm, almost too calm, thus in the proper state of mind to paint all that.

Letter to his mother, July 1890

LANDSCAPE AT AUVERS, 1890

First published in the United States in 1991 by Chronicle Books

Conceived, edited and designed by Russell Ash & Bernard Higton
Copyright © 1990 by Russell Ash & Bernard Higton

Printed in Hong Kong by Imago

ISBN 0-87701-809-X

10   9   8   7   6   5   4   3   2   1

Chronicle Books
275 Fifth Street
San Francisco, CA
94103

BOMC offers recordings and compact discs, cassettes
and records. For information and catalog write to
BOMR, Camp Hill, PA 17012.

Paintings in order of appearance: Musée d'Orsay, Paris/Scala; Musée
d'Orsay/Bridgeman; Private collection/Christie's; Hermitage Museum,
Leningrad/Scala; Musée d'Orsay/© Photo RMN; Rijksmuseum Kröller-
Müller, Otterlo; Rijksmuseum Kröller-Müller; Musée d'Orsay/© Photo
RMN; Gemeente Museum, The Hague/Artothek; Pushkin Museum, Moscow/
Scala; Kunstmuseum, Winterthur/Bridgeman; Musée d'Orsay/© Photo
RMN; Musée d'Orsay/Scala; Hermitage Museum/Scala; Musée d'Orsay/
Bulloz; Pushkin Museum/Scala.